Published by

Keith & Dufftown Railway Association,
Dufftown Station,
Dufftown
Banffshire AB55 4BA

www.keith-dufftown.org.uk

ISBN 0-9547346-1-0

Printed in Scotland by

W. Peters & Son Ltd
16 High Street, Turriff
AB53 4DT

Acknowledgements

I acknowledge the invaluable contributions made by the following people and organisations. Had it not been for the generous access given to their extensive photographic collections this book would not have been possible. I pay special tribute to those individuals who travelled extensively throughout the former Scottish Region of British Railways diligently recording the everyday scene before the Beeching Report wiped out these delightful country railways forever. Many of these people carried out most of their photography at weekends, often travelling considerable distances on overnight Friday into Saturday services to get to their chosen destinations. Some travelled by a mixture of train and scooter (this was in a time when the roads were not as busy as they are today!) These were the days when photography was by no means an easy hobby to finance so each photo had to count. It is to their credit that such a wealth of irreplaceable material is available today :

Douglas Hume
G.N.Turnbull
The Great North of Scotland Railway Association (G.N.S.R.A.) (The late Norris Forrest)
The late J.L.Stevenson
Hamish Stevenson
Fred Landery
Stuart W. Rankin
Martin Jenkins (Online Transport Archive)
Douglas Gray
Ian Johnstone

Keith Jones (G.N.S.R.A)
Maureen Webster (Keith & Dufftown Railway Association)

A special thanks to Robert Dey who prepared the map, gradient charts & signalling diagrams.

And thanks to Dr. Mike Cooper for his help in image preparation.

arts council for moray

The publisher, Keith & Dufftown Railway Association gratefully acknowledge the financial support received from Arts Council of Moray and HIE Moray.

HIE Moray

Introduction

The railway lines round the Moray coast were built between the years of 1846 & 1886. Elgin to Lossiemouth was the first portion to open on the 11th of August 1852. This was followed by the line from Grange (on the main Aberdeen / Keith Junction line) to Banff with a branch to Portsoy which opened on the 30th July 1859. It was some 25 years before Portsoy and Elgin were connected with the final section between Garmouth and Tochieneal being opened on the 1st of May1886.

There were significant engineering features required to carry the line round the coast most notably the large girder bridge over the River Spey and the trio of viaducts at Cullen made necessary by a diversion (requested by the Earl of Seafield) to the planned route. The summit of the line (476ft above sea level) was at Glenbarry with a long stiff climb of 1 in 70/1 in 72 on either side. Although predominantly single, short double line sections existed between Portessie & Buckie ($1^1/_4$ miles) and Grange North Junction & Cairnie Junction ($^1/_2$ mile). These remained until final closure.

With the advent of the Beeching Report the writing was on the wall for the railways of the coast with the Lossiemouth & Banff branches losing their passenger services in 6th April & 6th July 1964 respectively. The Lossiemouth branch was closed completely upon the withdrawal of goods services on the 28th March 1966. The remainder of the routes closed completely to both passenger and goods services on and from the 6th of May 1968 with track lifting commencing shortly thereafter. In the intervening years agriculture, house building and road improvement schemes have wiped out some of the old track bed. However, as well as the splendid viaducts at Garmouth and Cullen many parts of the route can still be found for those of us who are keen to find; and reflect upon; a way of life that has gone forever.

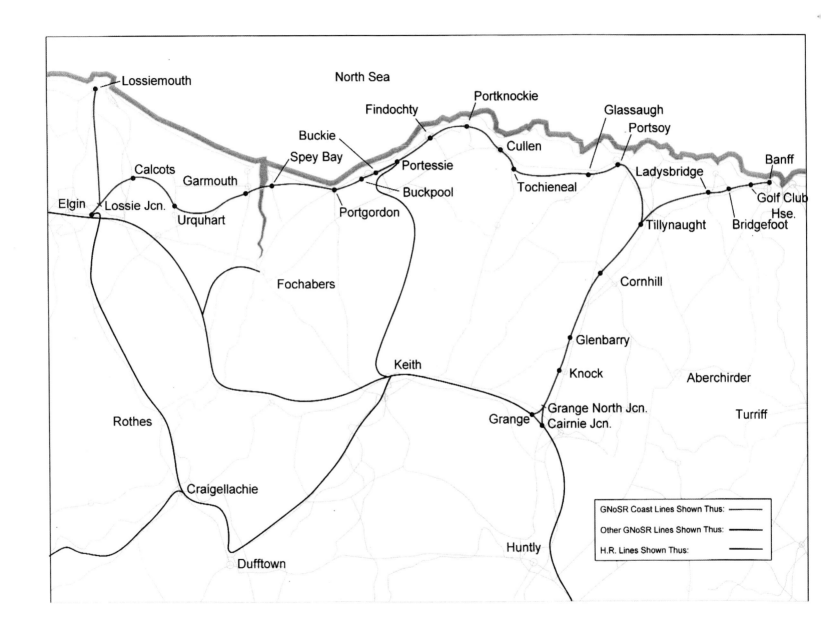

North Sea

Lossiemouth

Portknockie

Findochty

Glassaugh

Buckie

Portsoy

Spey Bay

Cullen

Banff

Calcots

Portessie

Ladysbridge

Garmouth

Golf Club

Elgin

Buckpool

Tochieneal

Lossie Jcn.

Hse.

Urquhart

Portgordon

Tillynaught

Bridgefoot

Fochabers

Cornhill

Glenbarry

Keith

Knock

Aberchirder

Rothes

Grange North Jcn.

Turriff

Grange

Cairnie Jcn.

Craigellachie

Huntly

Dufftown

GNoSR Coast Lines Shown Thus: ——————

Other GNoSR Lines Shown Thus: ——————

H.R. Lines Shown Thus: ——————

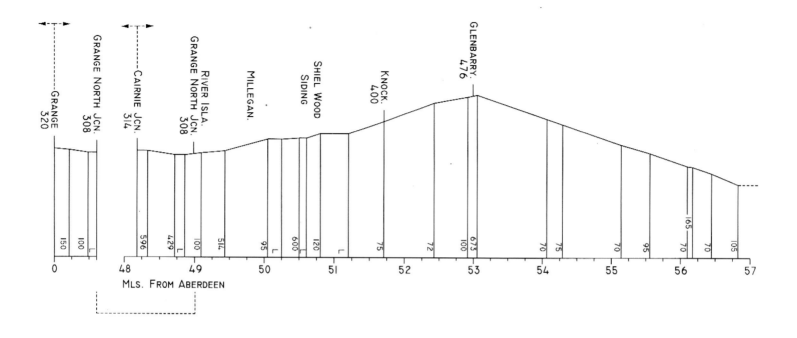

GRANGE 320
GRANGE NORTH JCN. 308
CAIRNIE JCN. 314
RIVER ISLA. GRANGE NORTH JCN. 308
MILLEGAN.
SHIEL WOOD SIDING
KNOCK. 400
GLENBARRY. 476

150 100 L   596 429 L 100 514   95 L   600 120 L   75   72 100 673   70 75   70 95   165 70 70 105

0   48   49   50   51   52   53   54   55   56   57

MLS. FROM ABERDEEN

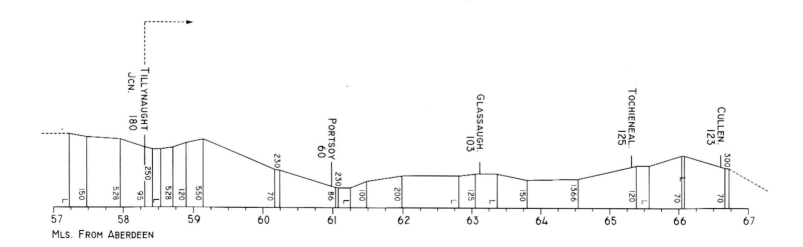

TILLYNAUGHT JCN. 180
PORTSOY 60
GLASSAUGH. 103
TOCHIENEAL. 125
CULLEN. 123

L 150 528 95 250 L 120 528 550   70 230   86 L 100 200   L 125 L 150 1366   120 L 70 300 L 70

57   58   59   60   61   62   63   64   65   66   67

MLS. FROM ABERDEEN

Gradient Charts

5

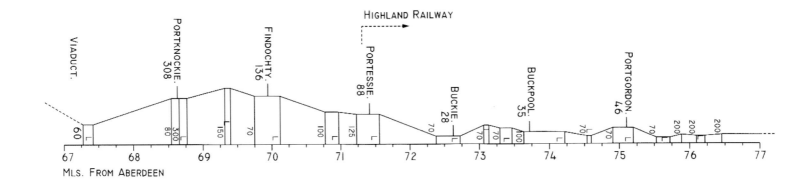

HIGHLAND RAILWAY

VIADUCT.

PORTKNOCKIE. 308

FINDOCHTY. 136

PORTESSIE. 88

BUCKIE. 28

BUCKPOOL. 35

PORTGORDON. 46

60 L 80 300 L 150 L 70 L 100 125 L 70 L 70 70 L 100 L 70 L 70 L 70 200 200 200

67 68 69 70 71 72 73 74 75 76 77

MLS. FROM ABERDEEN

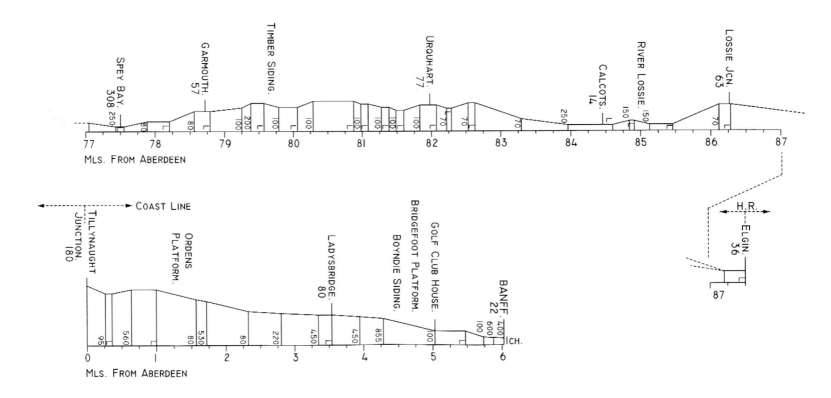

SPEY BAY. 308

GARMOUTH. 57

TIMBER SIDING.

URQUHART. 77

CALCOTS. 14

RIVER LOSSIE.

LOSSIE JCN. 63

250 80 L 80 L 100 200 L 100 L 100 L 100 100 100 L 100 70 L 70 L 70 250 L 150 L 150 L 70 L

77 78 79 80 81 82 83 84 85 86 87

MLS. FROM ABERDEEN

COAST LINE

TILLYNAUGHT JUNCTION. 180

ORDENS PLATFORM.

LADYSBRIDGE. 80

BRIDGEFOOT PLATFORM.

BOYNDIE SIDING.

GOLF CLUB HOUSE.

BANFF. 22

95 560 L 80 530 80 220 L 450 L 450 855 L 100 L 100 600 200 L ICH.

0 1 2 3 4 5 6

MLS. FROM ABERDEEN

H.R.

ELGIN. 36

87

Gradient Charts

Elgin (East) station, October 1967. From left to right are : In Platform 1 a two car Cravens Diesel Multiple Unit, in Platform 2 a BRCW Class 26 Type 2 Diesel waiting to depart with a Glen Line passenger train via Craigellachie and finally in Platform 4 another Type 2 on a passenger train for Aberdeen via the Coast Line. Elgin Centre signalbox (which, at the time of writing is still standing) can be seen in the distance on the left hand side of the photograph. Most of what can be seen here has vanished except for the main station building, thankfully this has been the subject of an excellent restoration project.

(Photo G.N.Turnbull)

ELGIN EAST

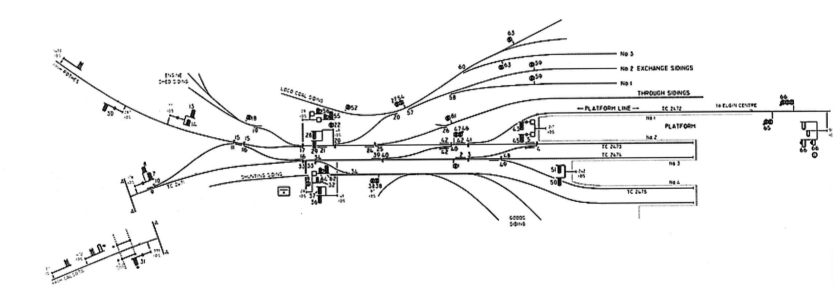

Elgin East Signalling Diagram

Elgin (East) signalbox in July 1967, where the Coast and Glen Lines diverge. The signalman can be seen looking out of the 'box window keeping an eye on the 'Signalbox Lad' who is about to hand over the single line key token for the section of line ahead. Elgin (East) was one of the larger signalboxes on the G.N.o S. system (Aberdeen North was the biggest). The track & signalling layout here allowed for trains to & from both the Glen & Coast routes to arrive and depart simultaneously. The Coast Line diverges to the left in the distance.

(Photo : G.N.Turnbull)

The 7.40am Elgin to Lossiemouth mixed (passenger & freight) train hauled by Kittybrewster Standard 2 (2-6-0) 78045 is leaving Elgin and on the approach to Pinefield level crossing. The date is the 13th of May 1961, not long before the advent of the diesels. A fast food outlet now occupies this spot.

(Photo : Douglas Hume)

Lossie Junction looking east with a down NBL Class 21 hauled coast service approaching in the distance. The Lossiemouth branch diverged to the left on the straight route. The distant (fishtail) signal arm below the branch signal was for Linksfield crossing gates.

(Photo ; N.Forrest/GNSRA)

A general view of Calcots station looking east taken from the now removed road bridge at the west end of the platforms. Note the vans stored in the small goods yard behind the station building. The signals are clear for an up train. Only part of the up platform remains of this idyllic scene today. (Photo : J.L.Stevenson)

The 12.30pm Elgin to Buckie Class 2 local service hauled by a Perth based Black 5 (45365) sweeps into Calcots station on the 4th of June 1960. Note the neat and tidy surroundings and the photographers overnight bag on the platform. 45365's fireman is preparing to hand the Lossie Junction token to the signalman. (Photo : Douglas Hume)

13

The main building on the eastbound platform at Calcots viewed from a westbound service in October 1967, seven months before final closure. The station is in need of a coat of paint and the hedge could benefit with a final trim before the onset of the last winter of operation.

(Photo : G.N.Turnbull)

The single platformed station at Urquhart on the 1st of August 1959 looking west. The goods yard appears to be used for the storage of wagons whilst on the platform the flower beds are well tended by Porter-in-Charge, Jimmy Brown. The station building and surrounding area served as a caravan park for a while after the lines were lifted. A private residence now occupies the site.   (Photo : Douglas Hume)

Garmouth station looking west on a sunny 4th June 1960. The well maintained permanent way and embankments are a credit to the local railwaymen. The Stationmasters house can be seen in the distance at the end of the platform. (Photo : Douglas Hume)

A Class 25 diesel hauled passenger train for Elgin crosses the Spey Viaduct between Garmouth & Spey Bay on the last day of passenger services (4th May 1968). (Photo : N.Forrest/GNSRA)

A drivers eye view of the Spey Viaduct between Garmouth and Spey Bay stations. The lattice post of Spey Bay's up distant signal, with arm removed is on the left. Thankfully this impressive structure still survives and forms part of a footpath between the two villages which local residents can now use officially, without the fear of being charged with trespassing...... (Photo : A.S.Clayton courtesy Online Transport Archive)

FOCHABERS
(SPEY BAY)

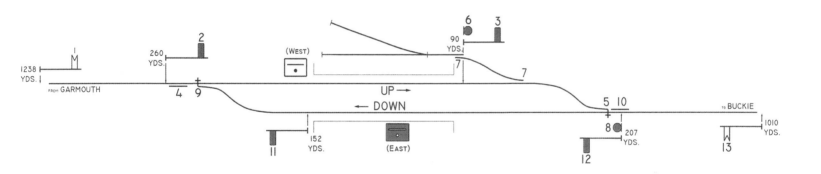

Spey Bay (Fochabers) Signalling Diagram

Spey Bay station looking east towards Buckie on the 1st of August 1959. Another fine example of a G.N.O.S. country station. The small signalbox on the left has been moved to the Keith & Dufftown Railway for restoration having spent the intervening years since the line was closed in a garden at Clochan near Buckie. (Photo : Douglas Hume)

Perth Black 5, 44959 calls at Spey Bay with the 9.30am Glasgow (Buchanan Street) to Elgin on the 1st of August 1959. The signalman deftly exchanges tokens with the fireman in an age old ritual that to all intents and purposes is now extinct on today's railway. A fine example of a L.N.E.R. staggered footbridge spans the gap between the two platforms. (Photo : Douglas Hume)

Kittybrewster B1, 61242 'Alexander Reith Gray' calls at Portgordon with the 12.30pm Elgin to Buckie local on the 1st August 1959. The Porter steps out briskly to deal with any disembarking passengers.   (Photo : Douglas Hume)

PORT GORDON

It is the 9th of June 1968 and Portgordon station has been closed for nearly 2 months now although you could almost be forgiven for thinking that a train may appear at any time.. Portgordon station was the location where German spies who had landed by U Boat during the Second World War were spotted and reported by the vigilant stationmaster when they attempted to purchase some travel tickets.

(Photo : G.N.Turnbull)

A fine study of the station building at Buckpool taken in February 1960 shortly before it was closed completely. Note the drinking fountain on the right hand side of the building.

(Photo : N.Forrest/GNSRA)

80113 calls at Buckpool with a Buckie to Elgin local passenger in February 1960.

(Photo : N.Forrest/GNSRA)

BUCKIE

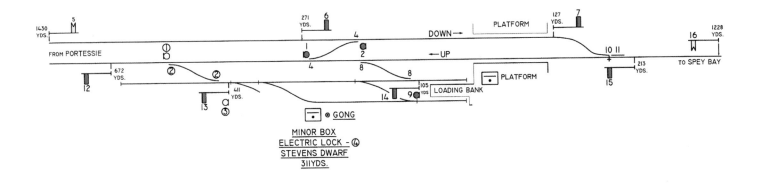

GONG - 17
SPACES - 18
ELECTRIC RELEASE TO MINOR BOX - 3

STEVENS & SONS O.P. 5 1/4 FRAME
18 LEVERS
DIAGRAM DATE: 9/9/39

Buckie Signalling Diagram

A Class 26 Type 2 diesel hauled passenger train from Aberdeen to Elgin clatters into Buckie as the secondman picks up the Calcots single line key token from the signalman. It is October 1967, seven months remain before final closure.
(Photo : G.N.Turnbull)

A splendid view of Buckie looking east towards Portessie (date unknown). The signalman and an intending passenger exchange gossip at the signalbox window. The large two wheeled barrow on the eastbound platform has some parcels traffic for the next up service. There is also evidence of plenty goods traffic in the yard. The line was double track between here and Portessie just over one mile away.

(Photo : J. L. Stevenson)

The east end of Buckie taken after closure and before the demolition gangs arrived. The shunting frame, which controlled the east connection to the goods yard, is on the right. The long loading bank was the scene of high activity when the fishing fleet came in and all traffic went by rail to the London markets. (Photo : N.Forrest/GNSRA)

PORTESSIE

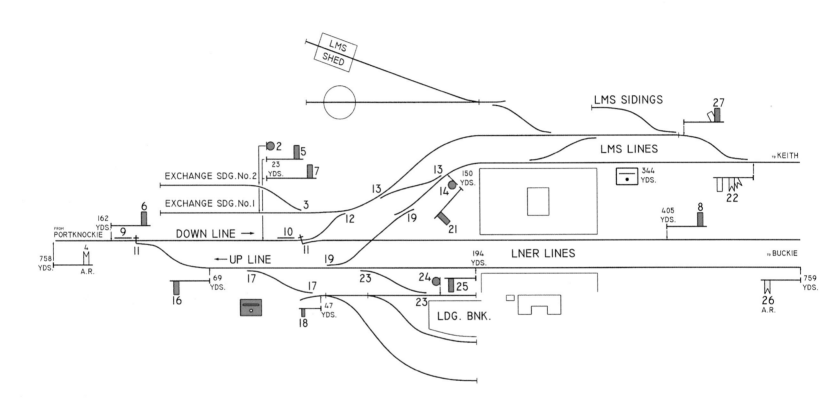

SPARE-1-20
SPACE-28
STEVENS 51/4" FRAME
DIAGRAM DATE: 9/9/39

Portessie Signalling Diagram

West and eastbound Diesel Multiple Units (Swindon Cross Country 3 car set on the left and Cravens 2 car unit on the right) side by side at Portessie on the last day of passenger services around the Coast : 4th May 1968 (Photo : Fred Landery)

Portessie looking east when the Highland Railway connection & signalling were still in situ. Note the interesting mix of Great North of Scotland & Highland Railway signals in this rare view. The Highland two road engine shed can be seen behind the station sign. The stone base of the water column is still there today.

(Photo : J. L. Stevenson collection)

Keith based Class 2P 4-4-0 (40622) accelerates away downhill from Portessie on the double line towards Buckie. The date is the 13th of August 1960 and this is the 3.45pm Aberdeen to Elgin. The former Highland Line from Keith via Enzie came in behind the fence on the right hand side.
(Photo : Douglas Hume)

A sunlit view of the main building on the eastbound side at Portessie with plenty to see for those interested in platform furniture. This view was taken in September 1963. I wonder where the totem station sign is now? (Photo : G.N.Turnbull)

A fine detailed shot of a standard LNER rail built footbridge at Portessie (which replaced an earlier GNoSR wooden structure). The former HR platform can be seen on the right.

(Photo : N.Forrest/GNSRA)

Findochty station looking east on that miserably wet last day of passenger train services (4th of May 1968). A group of youngsters are probably about to make their last railway journey from their local station. Some period cars can be seen in the car park behind the fence.

(Photo : Fred Landery)

The 2.15pm Aberdeen to Elgin departs from Portknockie on the 4th of June 1960 hauled by Perth Black 5, 44961. There is little trace left of this station today.
(Photo ; Douglas Hume)

A fine view of the westerly approaches to Cullen and its brace of magnificent viaducts, the longest one of eight arches being most prominent. There were plans to demolish this structure in the early seventies as part of a road improvement scheme but thankfully local opposition to this proposal prevailed and this splendid legacy of a bygone railway age is still with us. (Photo : N.Forrest/GNSRA)

A lofty view of the Seatown from the famous Cullen viaduct. Has the Seatown changed very much? (Photo : G.N.Turnbull)

Black 5 44961 (see page 37) arrives at Cullen on the 4th of June 1960. The station flowerbeds reflect a great pride in the job. What a pleasure it must have been to wait for a train here on a warm summer afternoon.

(Photo : Douglas Hume)

Cullen station on the 10th of June 1968. With complete closure some 2 months earlier the first signs of decay are beginning to set in. Like most of the Coastal stations little trace can now be found that it ever existed. (Photo : G.N. Turnbull)

Tochieneal station, crossing loop & signalbox looking west. Although the signalbox & goods yard were still operational at the time this picture was taken the passenger station had been closed since October 1951. Note the water column on the right.　　(Photo : N. Forrest/GNSRA)

PORTSOY

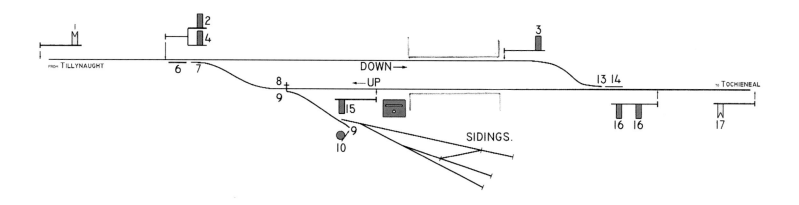

Portsoy Signalling Diagram

A general view of the passenger station at Portsoy looking towards Tillynaught. The disused down platform still remains in excellent condition despite not having seen a passenger train for nearly 8 years.

(Photo : N. Forrest/GNSRA)

Reflecting his great affection for the Black 5 the photographer catches 44698 arriving at Portsoy with the 2.30pm Aberdeen to Elgin on the 13th of August 1960. Although the crossing loop is still intact it is now out of use with the signalbox having been closed almost a year earlier on the 22nd of August 1959. Nevertheless the disused platform is still kept in good order. (Photo : Douglas Hume)

Almost identical in design to Cullen the main building at Portsoy is captured in this October 1967 shot. This building still survives in pleasant surroundings.

(Photo : G.N.Turnbull)

An Elgin to Aberdeen service calls at Portsoy. Although no longer functioning as a signalbox the structure still seems to serve some purpose as a Permanent Way Inspectors Office perhaps?

(Photo : G.N.Turnbull)

TILLYNAUGHT JUNCTION

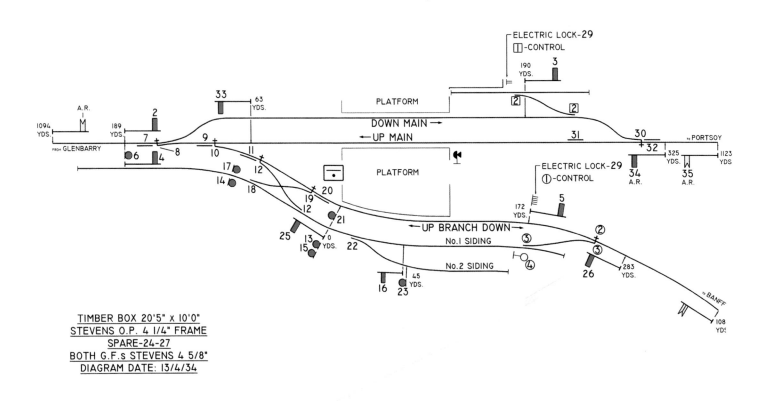

TIMBER BOX 20'5" x 10'0"
STEVENS O.P. 4 1/4" FRAME
SPARE-24-27
BOTH G.F.s STEVENS 4 5/8"
DIAGRAM DATE: 13/4/34

Tillynaught Junction Signalling Diagram

The 3.45pm Aberdeen to Elgin arrives at Tillynaught on the 20th August 1960. Class 4 2-6-4T 80121 was one of two such machines allocated to Keith Junction shed. The large station building had lost most of its original canopy by this time but was nevertheless still impressive for a country junction station.

(Photo : Douglas Hume)

The station sign says it all. A Cairnie Junction bound Cravens diesel unit arrives from Elgin to pick up passengers who have just arrived from Banff. The steam hauled branch passenger patiently waits for some trade before returning to the terminus. (Photo : G.N.Turnbull)

A general view of the Junction station buildings at Tillynaught. The canopy on the main building was still in place at this time. Freight traffic for Banff is stabled in the siding on the extreme right.　　　　　　　　　　　　　　　　　　　　　(Photo : Hamish Stevenson collection)

A holiday special working from Banff to Glasgow Buchanan Street pulls away from Tillynaught on the 1st August 1959 with Class K2 61782 in charge. The rural location of the junction station can be appreciated in this view. (Photo : Douglas Hume)

Cornhill station on a wintry 6th of April 1968, four weeks before final closure. Coal wagons in the small yard indicate some freight business that survived to the end.

(Photo : Douglas Hume)

GLENBARRY

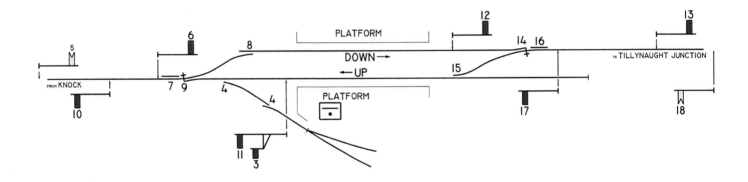

PLATFORM

DOWN →

← UP

PLATFORM

FROM KNOCK

TO TILLYNAUGHT JUNCTION

16 WORKING
2 SPACES
18 TOTAL

REV.0.

Glenbarry Signalling Diagram

54

The neat Type 2a signalbox at Glenbarry taken in the earlier part of the summer of 1966. Glenbarry signalbox was taken out of use on the 25th of June 1966. You can just see that the goods yard has already been lifted having been closed on the 2nd of November 1964.

(Photo : KDRA/Ian Johnstone)

Glenbarry looking towards Knock & Cairnie Junction. The signals are cleared for an up train and the signalman is leaving the cabin to meet its iminient arrival. It would appear that economies have meant that the platform edges are not fully white lined.

(Photo : N.Forrest/GNSRA)

KNOCK

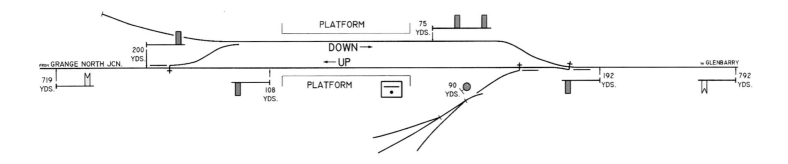

PLATFORM   75 YDS.

DOWN →

FROM GRANGE NORTH JCN.

← UP

200 YDS.

719 YDS.

108 YDS.

PLATFORM

90 YDS.

192 YDS.

TO GLENBARRY

792 YDS.

13 WORKING
3 SPACES
16 TOTAL

1894

Knock Signalling Diagram

Knock station looking towards Aberdeen on the 6th of April 1968. Like Cornhill, freight traffic continued here (from the adjacent distillery) right up to final closure. The distillery is still there but all that remains of the station is the passenger platform and goods loading bank, even the road bridge has been levelled.

(Photo : Douglas Hume)

58

GRANGE NORTH

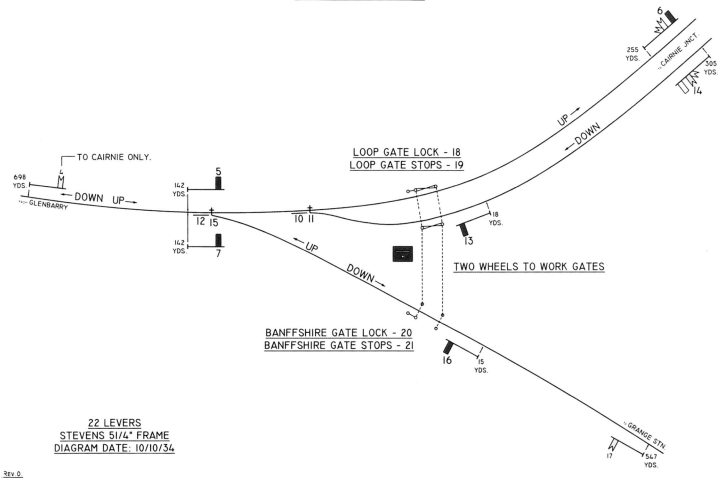

LOOP GATE LOCK - 18
LOOP GATE STOPS - 19

TO CAIRNIE ONLY.

698 YDS.

FROM GLENBARRY

← DOWN   UP →

142 YDS.

5

12 15

142 YDS.

7

10 11

← UP

DOWN →

255 YDS.

TO CAIRNIE JNCT.

6

UP →

← DOWN

305 YDS.

14

18 YDS.

13

TWO WHEELS TO WORK GATES

BANFFSHIRE GATE LOCK - 20
BANFFSHIRE GATE STOPS - 21

16   15 YDS.

TO GRANGE STN.

17   547 YDS.

22 LEVERS
STEVENS 51/4" FRAME
DIAGRAM DATE: 10/10/34

REV. 0.

Grange North Junction Signalling Diagram

59

CRANGE NORTH

Grange North Junction signalbox photographed after complete closure. As well as controlling, at one time, two level crossings, it also formed the northern part of the triangle between itself, Grange Station and Cairnie Junction on the main line. Steam locomotives could be reversed here if they were too long for the Keith turntable or if a test trip was required after any running repairs at the shed.   (Photo : Douglas Gray)

CAIRNIE JUNCTION

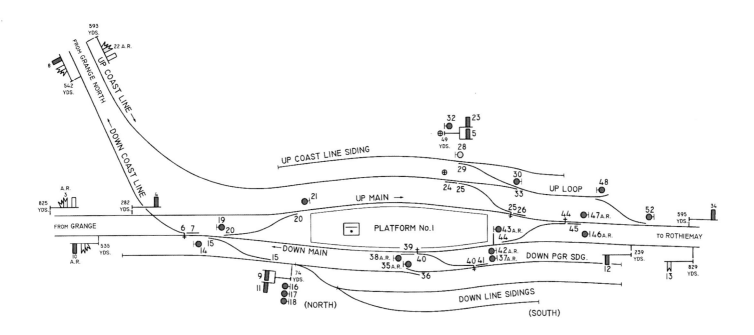

STEVENS & SONS O.P. 5 1/4 FRAME
52 LEVERS
DIAGRAM DATE: 10/10/34

REV.I.

Cairnie Junction Signalling Diagram

The lofty Type1 signalbox at Cairnie Junction photographed after closure and before demolition. The building had a slight lean to one side in its later years. Cairnie Junction was purely an exchange platform. (Photo : Douglas Gray)

The 9.30am Elgin to Aberdeen (via Buckie) arrives at Cairnie Junction on the 2nd of June 1960. The unusual arrangement at Cairnie can been seen developing in this view. When the 9.30 had cleared the points in the foreground it was then signalled back and coupled up to the coaches already in the right hand platform (which had previously arrived from Elgin via Dufftown). The combined train then proceeded to Aberdeen. The 9.30 is being hauled by B1 61346. The Black 5 (45365) in the left (westbound) platform will have just worked the passenger from Elgin via Dufftown.

(Photo : Douglas Hume)

It is over seven years later now and the passenger train from the Coast is now hauled by Type 2 Class 26 D5333. It will still be signalled back into the platform line in the foreground before heading to Aberdeen, however there are no coaches to couple onto now. The passenger train from the route via Dufftown is the Cravens unit in the storage siding on the right. This train has terminated at Cairnie and will return to Elgin either via the Coast or via Dufftown after the next westbound service from Aberdeen calls to transfer passengers.　　(Photo : G.N.Turnbull)

GRANGE.

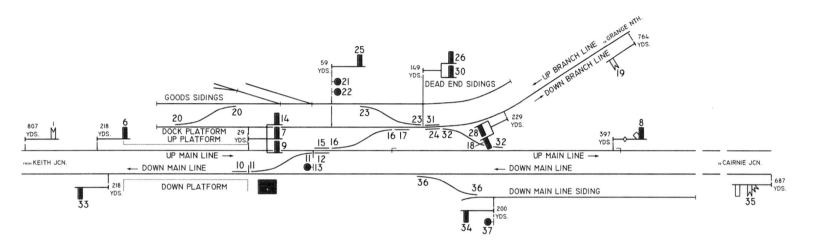

40 LEVERS
STEVENS 5I/4" FRAME
DIAGRAM DATE: 10/10/1934

Rev.I.

Grange Station Signalling Diagram

Grange station on the west side of the Grange 'triangle'. Little trace now remains of this tidy and well kept station. Photograph taken on the 15th August 1959.
(Photo : Douglas Hume)

A North British Type 2 Class 21 waits for the signal at Lossiemouth with a mixed train for Elgin. (Photo : N.Forrest/GNSRA)

(Photo : Douglas Hume)

Lossiemouth before and after shots: The 1.44pm up passenger for Elgin is ready for departure hauled by 78045 on the 13th of May 1961.

Just over 5 years later and both train & tracks have gone.

(Photo : S.W.Rankin)

The derelict signalbox at Lossiemouth after tracklifting and the inevitable vandalism that follows. Lossiemouth signalbox was one of the first to have electric lighting installed.

(Photo : S.W.Rankin)

September 1963 and a Banff bound passenger train calls at Ladysbridge. The Porter-in-charge looks out for some trade. (Photo ; G.N.Turnbull)

78045 calls at Ladysbridge with the 4pm Banff to Tillynaught service on the 20th of August 1960. The small goods yard awaits some business. The Banff passenger service was steam hauled until the end, apparently because of some difficulty in working a mixed (goods & passenger formation) train with the diesels available at that time .

(Photo : Douglas Hume)

71

The G.N.o.S. lower quadrant home signal protecting Blairshinnoch main road level crossing between Bridgefoot Halt and Ladysbridge. The distant (lower) signal arm is for Ladysbridge station level crossing. (Photo : Douglas Hume)

Bridgefoot Halt looking west on the 6th of July 1964.

(Photo : Douglas Hume)

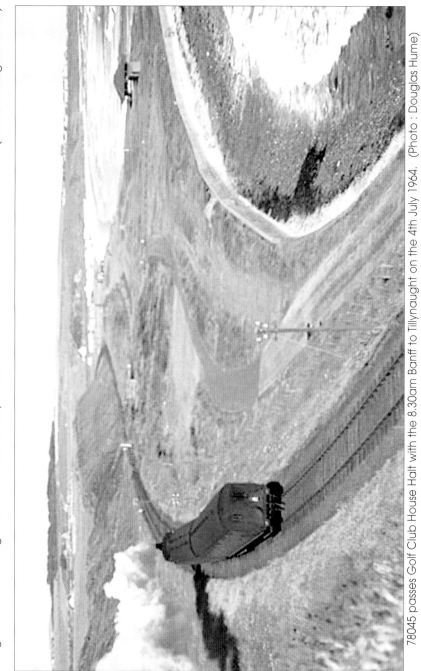

78045 passes Golf Club House Halt with the 8.30am Banff to Tillynaught on the 4th July 1964. (Photo : Douglas Hume)

BANFF

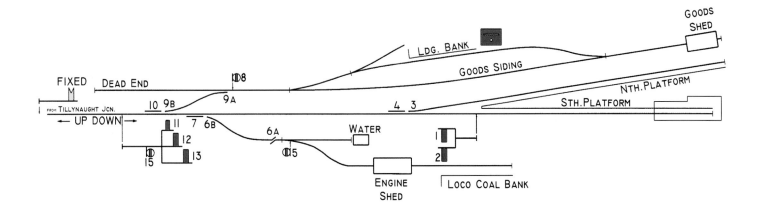

FIXED
M
DEAD END

FROM TILLYNAUGHT JCN.

← UP DOWN →

LDG. BANK

GOODS SIDING

GOODS
SHED

NTH. PLATFORM

STH. PLATFORM

WATER

ENGINE
SHED

LOCO COAL BANK

15 LEVERS
No.14 SPARE

DIAGRAM DATE: 1929

REV.0.

1959

Banff Signalling Diagram

2P 0-4-4T 55185 shunts at Banff on the 1st of August 1959. The signalbox is still in operation. Note the engine shed with a supply of coal wagons on the left to replenish the loco tender.

(Photo : Douglas Hume)

78045 takes on water in this general view of the terminus at Banff on the 20th August 1960. Note the coal wagon positioned to replenish the tender in front of the water tower. It will be noted that the signalbox is still in situ although by this time it was no longer in use having closed on the 29th of May 1960. There appears to be a healthy amount of goods traffic in the cramped yard. Note the three way set of points in the foreground no doubt necessary due to the limitations of available space.   (Photo : Douglas Hume)

The interior of the trainshed at Banff in September 1963. Judging by the general condition of the interior it would appear that no steam engine ventured as far as the buffer stop?

(Photo : G.N.Turnbull)

The last day of passenger train services and the Driver & Fireman pose beside their engine, 4th June 1964 (Photo : Douglas Gray)

It is Saturday the 4th of May 1968 and the remains of Banff station await the final goods train which will uplift all wagons on the following Wednesday before returning to Keith Junction (via Buckie).

(Photo : Fred Landery)

British Railways — Scottish Region

TRANSPORT ACT, 1962

WITHDRAWAL OF
RAILWAY PASSENGER SERVICES

The British Railways Board hereby give notice, in accordance with Section 56 (7) of the Transport Act, 1962, that on and from 2nd DECEMBER, 1963, they propose to discontinue all railway passenger services

BETWEEN

BANFF
AND
TILLYNAUGHT

AND FROM THE FOLLOWING STATIONS:—

BANFF, GOLF CLUB HOUSE HALT
BRIDGEFOOT HALT,
LADYSBRIDGE and ORDENS HALT

It appears to the Board that the following alternative services will be available:—

BY ROAD:—

Operator—W. ALEXANDER & SONS (Northern) LIMITED

Service	Service
No. 9 (Route 5) ABERDEEN-BANFF	No. 34 (Route 5) INVERNESS-ABERDEEN (Coast Route) via Elgin, Buckie, Banff and Macduff
No. 10 (Route 5a) ABERDEEN-BUCKIE via Turriff, Macduff and Banff	No. 53 (Route 5c) BANFF-TURRIFF via Mountblairy and Scotston
No. 13 (Route 5) ABERDEEN-BANFF-MACDUFF via Aberchirder	No. 54 (Route 24) BANFF-HUNTLY via Cornhill and Aberchirder

Any user of the rail service at any station from which it is proposed to withdraw ALL passenger services and any body representing such users, desirous of objecting to the proposal, may lodge objections within six weeks of 14th SEPTEMBER, 1963, i.e. not later than 28th OCTOBER, 1963, addressing any objections to the Secretary of the Transport Users' Consultative Committee for Scotland at 39 George Street, Edinburgh, 2.

NOTE:—If any objections are lodged within the period specified above, the closure cannot be proceeded with until the Transport Users' Consultative Committee has reported to the Minister of Transport and the Minister has given his consent (Section 56 (8) of the Transport Act, 1962).

Published by British Railways (Scottish Region) B.R. 35012 · B 36510 · K · August, 1963

Printed in Great Britain by McCorquodale, Glasgow

Closure notice Banff branch. (Photo : G.N.Turnbull)

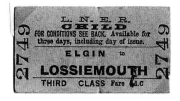

L.N.E.R S.S. 8195 5,000 8/31 (F1).   M 9801

LUGGAGE.

From_____

To BANFF

Great North of Scotland Railway.

LUGGAGE.

TILLYNAUGHT JUNC.

From.....................................

L.N.E.R.

LUGGAGE

From ....

To CULLEN

Great North of Scotland Railway.

LUGGAGE.

Portnockie

From ....

Est M2571 1M. 1/33   M.9801

L.N.E.R.

LUGGAGE.

From

To CORNHILL

Tickets & Luggage Labels

Postcript

It is interesting to note that Ministerial consent to close the main coast route was very slow in coming, in fact some might say it was a very close thing. Plans were already in preparation not only to single the main Aberdeen to Keith line but also to keep the portion between Cairnie Junction and either Huntly or Keith Junction to be used as two single lines - one for the existing Aberdeen / Inverness line and one for the coast. Cairnie Junction would have been done away with and signalboxes would have been retained at Grange North (gate box only) Tillynaught and Buckie. But for a signature on a piece of Government paper the call just could have been 'Huntly, change for the Coast'.

Well, we can only reflect on what might have been.........

Fort William
December 2005

Contact Information

Keith & Dufftown Railway Association

Dufftown Railway Station
Dufftown
Banffshire
AB55 4BA

Great North of Scotland Railway Association

The Membership Secretary
Graighall Cottage
Guildtown
Perth
PH2 6DF